Kitchen Kulture

gestalten

THE EVOLUTION OF THE KITCHEN: FROM BACKSTAGE TO CENTER STAGE

by

Noelia Hobeika

It's 1959, at the height of the Cold War. Khrushchev and Nixon are standing next to the model of a typical American kitchen arguing over which of their respective systems is superior, communism or capitalism. The backdrop of this famous televised dispute, which would become known as the Kitchen Debate, couldn't have been more appropriate: kitchens mirror the societies they were built in like no other space in a household.

At its most basic use as the place for food preparation, the kitchen has not fundamentally changed. Yet over the course of the twentieth century, everything else about it underwent immense transformation. From its location within a home to its scale, today's kitchen is a far cry from its precursors. It has turned into the hub of the house; a place for social gathering, collaborative cooking, event hosting, and communal dining. The epitome of a multi-functional space (often with its own stereo system and television set), the kitchen has also become the architect and interior designer's favorite room, as it provides endless opportunities to experiment with innovative design and technology.

For a very long time, the kitchen was seen as a service area that was relegated to the back of the house, hidden away from the main living spaces where eating and socializing took place. As better ventilation and sanitation became available after the First World War, design professionals started to pay more attention to the kitchen. At the same time, however, the post-war years also saw many negative developments such as inflation and a housing crisis.

In response to this situation, the city of Frankfurt am Main in Germany initiated a social housing program in 1926 known as the New Frankfurt, and commissioned Margarete Schütte-Lihotzky (Austria's first female architect) to conceive a practical, compact kitchen that would fit the modern affordable home. Based on contemporary theories about hygiene and productivity, Schütte-Lihotzky's design, dubbed the Frankfurt Kitchen, was fully-equipped and aimed to optimize efficiency. It became the standard model for over such as "If you don't have enough time, maybe you don't have enough Tappan Time Machines."

The ever-expanding range of up-to-the-minute kitchen products offered to the consumer was displayed in shopping malls, a space that perfectly embodied post-war America's capitalist values as defended by Nixon during the Kitchen Debate. Beyond ideology, kitchen designs and advertisements continued to echo social attitudes toward domesticity, mainly catering to the housewife. Indeed, slogans similar to Tappan's were targeting married, stay-at-home suburban mothers. Europe caught up quickly with the United States with brands such as Braun, which developed entire kitchen appliance collections that were coveted and distributed worldwide.

Not everyone was enthralled with this commercial abundance, though. In the 1960s, a group of politically engaged and socially minded artists, mostly from Britain and the United States, produced art that aimed to denounce the modern kitchen as an emblem of wasteful consumer culture and retrograde social conformity. Feminists also criticized the domestic ideals that were encouraged and reinforced by designs like that of the Frankfurt Kitchen, which was said to seclude women in both physical and psychological ways.

While the kitchen continued to expand, some people were convinced that the convenience food industry would render cooking, and thereby the kitchen, obsolete. In a book by Molly Harrison published in 1972 titled *The Kitchen in History*, the kitchen of the future—before supposedly going extinct—was imagined to be a compact work station in the shape of a cylinder with all appliances and equipment tightly fitting together in a manner suitable for a spaceship.

Experimental thinking was the hallmark of the 1970s, giving rise to alternative kitchen designs. Environmental concerns were factored into the choice of materials, and sustainable kitchen devices such as the solar cooker were invented. Other design professionals tackled another type of self-sufficiency, designing kitchen tools specifically for the use of the elderly and the disabled.

From the 1980s onwards, the kitchen expanded even further. Open-plan layouts that integrated the kitchen with other living spaces became more common as a result of the loft culture that had developed over the previous decade. Originally, lofts were derelict factories

10,000 homes in Frankfurt, and inspired countless kitchen units in apartments around the world thereafter.

The Frankfurt Kitchen was the result of extensive reserach by Schütte-Lihotzky in the form of timemotion studies and interviews with women, which ultimately led her to design a narrow kitchen layout often compared to a factory conveyor belt. Each prefabricated kitchen came complete with a swivel stool, an adjustable ceiling lamp, a gas stove, a foldable ironing board, and a sink. The layout was meant to reduce the time women spent cooking and cleaning and free them either for work or leisure, both of which promoted economic growth.

In the decades that followed, the kitchen evolved from a purely utilitarian, space-saving room into a bigger, brighter area with more design potential. The 1930s and 1940s continued to favor smaller kitchens, but a trend towards new fashionable tile colors, countertop materials, and technologically advanced appliances was already emerging. The iconic black-and-white checkered kitchen floor became popular during this time.

By the 1950s and 1960s, kitchens were full-blown style and status statements. As the United States came to dominate the world market in consumer goods after the Second World War, many more shopping choices were made available to customers, with kitchens and their gadgets being no exception. Pastel-colored enamel appliances were all the rage, and owning the latest toaster, fridge, and later microwave became a means to assert a certain social status. Brands such as General Electric and Tappan created strong corporate identities and took advantage of the new medium of television advertising to promote slogans

> IN THE 1970s, THE KITCHEN OF THE FUTURE WAS IMAGINED TO BE A COMPACT WORK STATION SUITABLE FOR A SPACESHIP.
<<

family. Kitchens are now often the biggest rooms in the house, easily allowing for collaborative cooking. Beyond being the setting for food preparation, the kitchen, given its extended size and added devices such as televisions, sound systems, and Wi-Fi, has developed into an enjoyable site for leisure, hosting, and work: the twenty-first century kitchen is the new living room, dining room, and office wrapped into one space.

From a hidden staging area, the kitchen has evolved into a full-blown stage to show off culinary savoir-faire. Cooking is no longer seen as the preparation phase of a dinner party—it *is* the party. It has become a social act that guests participate in, and the kitchen table has consequently morphed into a more casual dining table. Food has always brought people together, but today's kitchen reinforces this community aspect by inciting friends and family to congregate not only to eat the food but to prepare it as well.

The fact that people are spending more time and money on their kitchen additionally stems from the current foodie culture. The foodie craze—as witnessed through the countless cooking shows on television and the endless stream of picture-perfect food imagery on social networks—encourages people to lead a healthier lifestyle by paying closer attention to the food they eat. As a result, everyone fancies themselves a gourmet and wants the kitchen that proves it. As our world becomes ever more fast-paced,

with few residential amenities that had been taken over by artists and converted into both living and working spaces. Over time, though, lofts became fashionable and were adopted as living quarters beyond the urban art scene. People were attracted to the creative and unconventional lifestyle that came to be associated with lofts. Their lack of defined structure and their significant size inspired a playful sense of freedom, leading residents to break unspoken conventions and rethink the possible dynamics of a home. Cooking was also increasingly seen as a fun, creative endeavor rather than a chore.

Designers began to approach the kitchen as a more malleable space, generating equipment that was multi-functional, aesthetically pleasing, and hyper-efficient all at once. German kitchen manufacturer bulthaup was a notable part of this trend. Their kitchen workbench launched in 1988 exemplifies the decade's forward-thinking designs that are still relevant today. An adaptable island model, the workbench and its three parts—cooktop, water point, and worktop—could be adjusted according to taste and individual requirements such as height. The media proclaimed it was the first real innovation in kitchen design since the Frankfurt Kitchen.

Today's kitchen continues to reflect contemporary thoughts on domesticity, food, and technology. Far from being the housewife's domain, the kitchen is more than ever a place for the entire foodie culture urges us to slow down and take more time to prepare our meals instead of opting for the easier ready-to-eat or take-out solutions.

With regard to technology, new kitchen designs also mirror another current trend: outdoor living. Designers are devising kitchen equipment that is adapted for the outdoors—and more sophisticated than the food truck. Think portable picnic appliances or mobile bread-making units. Sustainability continues to be of significant concern in these designs and, more broadly, the kitchen has become a laboratory for new materials and power sources.

This book shines a light on today's most striking examples of kitchens that are testing grounds for environmentally-friendly innovation, and lively spaces inspiring a higher quality of life by prompting better eating habits and bringing together family and friends. Most of the featured photographs are of kitchens in private homes, custom-made to fit with their owners' personalities and living quarters. From a vast, open-plan kitchen in a London townhouse to a kitchenette inside a student studio in Berlin, the professionals behind these designs uncover the full potential of the twenty-first century kitchen—that is so much more than a kitchen.

>>

COOKING IS NO LONGER SEEN AS THE PREPARATION PHASE OF A DINNER PARTY— IT *IS* THE PARTY.

<<

VIPP KITCHEN
Copenhagen, Denmark
Morten Bo Jensen for Vipp

Vipp began making pedal bins in the 1930s. More recently, it started designing furniture for the room most likely to surround its pedal bin: the kitchen. Seeing as the company has over 70 years of experience in working with stainless steel, it was only logical that its kitchen modules should be made of that material. The industrial look is in keeping with the original bin, and the robust metal has a long life ahead of it. Vipp offers its modules in either white or black, and in different shapes and sizes.

>>

FUNCTION-ALITY, LONGEVITY, AND A CONSISTENT AESTHETIC.

<<

VIPP KITCHEN PRODUCTS

Copenhagen, Denmark

Morten Bo Jensen for Vipp

Danish company Vipp, whose original pedal bin from 1939 is included in MoMA's Architecture and Design collection in New York, today makes many products for the home, maintaining an emphasis on functionality, longevity, and a consistent aesthetic language. Its kitchen range is no exception: even in something as small as the salt and pepper mills, the swivel tops are cast in solid stainless steel, while the aluminum base is lined with rubber for stability and protection of other surfaces. The trivet set and porcelain vessels, designed with ceramicist Annemette Kissow, echo this attention to detail and simplicity.

MANO

Vildbjerg, Denmark

Kvik

The smooth white surfaces of Kvik's Mano kitchen range work beautifully when teamed with the coarse wood of a rustic table. Industrial-inspired lighting brings a third style into play, and each element holds its own while also forming a unified whole. The Mano range can be combined with Kvik's Sociable Kitchen concept. The idea is to create a multi-functional kitchen with a spacious island at its center where family and friends can come together to cook, talk, laugh, and simply enjoy being in each other's company.

MATRYOSHKA

Turin, Italy

Andrea Marcante, Adelaide Testa / UdA Architects

Though tucked by necessity into a small corner of this Turin apartment, UdA's Matryoshka kitchen packs a very polished punch. A wealth of visual textures sets off the kitchen from the other spaces, all of which feature their own very distinct architecture. The bold diagonal lines of the overhead units are punctuated by a marbled panel and create a striking counterpoint to the color blocking of the units below. A slanted black-lacquer base, itself a rigid geometric shape, engages with the graphic pattern on the wallpaper and allows the kitchen to merge with the overall context of its surroundings.

DESIGN LINE

Gusterath-Tal, Germany

Supergrau
produced by Nomad Kitchen Cubes

A collaboration between two German design firms, the Nomad DESIGN LINE weds the unitary system of the Nomad Kitchen Cubes with the sustainable approach and light aesthetics of Supergrau. Using recoverable materials and smart technologies, the range includes a sink with tap and handle in white Corian, a bleached maple shelf, and a unit with integrated heat lamps. The units, built on smooth-rolling casters, can be easily recombined into different configurations for temporary or evolving needs and spaces.

TRAY

Stege, Denmark

Christina Liljenberg Halstrøm
for DESIGN NATION

A sheet of steel, two ash-wood rods, and four rubber bands are all that go into making this dapper tray. Deconstruction and reconstruction are simple, which means it is easy to replace broken parts and keep waste to a minimum. The subdued colors (it comes in green, light gray, and black) dispense with all things fancy and leave the task of decoration to whatever you choose to carry on it—be that movie-night snacks, a posh TV dinner, or afternoon tea and cake.

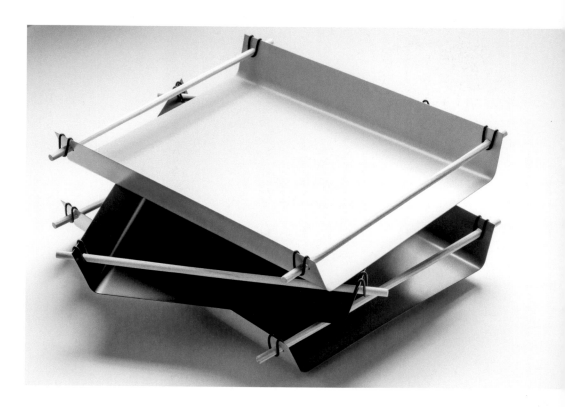

GAMMA KITCHEN COLLECTION

Milan, Italy

Arclinea

Gamma by Arclinea is an exceptionally modern kitchen concept that is now part of the Arclinea collection. It provides straightforward, flexible solutions for the most diverse design needs. The units reflect the company's core values—quality, functionality, customization, and socializing—and give you an almost endless variety of worktops, finishes, and door styles to choose from. Gamma can also be used in lounges, bedrooms, and bathrooms, which means you can bring these spaces into visual harmony with the most important room in the home.

ATELIER KITCHEN HAIDACHER

Perca, Italy

Lukas Mayr

Once used by the Haidacher family carpentry as a workshop building, this small hut in South Tyrol was reinvented as a 21st century kitchen showroom. Under the gabled roof, architect Lukas Mayr created a single interior volume, burnished entirely in light-absorbing black resin. All focus is drawn to an enormous block in the middle, a kitchen island built in cherry wood with sterling silver elements and highlighted with pendant lamps. Mayr's design exercises restraint, whittling the concept of "kitchen" down to the idea of a gathering point rendered in warm, natural materials.

CONVERSION OF OLD STONEHOUSE

Scaiano, Switzerland

wespi de meuron romeo architects
produced by Reto Vanzo Schreinerei

The renovation of this historic house in Scaiano, on the Swiss-Italian border, raises the interior to contemporary standards of comfort while emphasizing the archaic simplicity of the original stone walls. Glass and larch wood framing give onto vistas of the stunning Lago Maggiore. The kitchen counter is designed as an extension of the concrete staircase, and is set over a series of wooden cabinets. An inset fireplace and overhead lighting reduce the need for additional furniture.

ESTATE IN EXTREMADURA

Cáceres, Spain

Camino Alonso / ÁBATON Arquitectura
produced by ELMAR

Once an abandoned stable, this building in the Spanish country-side is now a family home that respects the environment, combines the old with the new, and understands that cooking can bring everyone—even teenagers and their parents—together. The kitchen and dining area takes up a large share of the living space and opens on to the lawn by the pool. Incorporating the overall style of the house, it features a mixture of well-worn stone, weathered wood, modern concrete, and iron beams. Floor-to-ceiling windows flood the space with sunlight and make the huge dining table (plenty of space for guests) an attractive place for kids to do homework and chat with Mom and Dad while dinner gets under way.

AN AMSTERDAM APARTMENT

Duivendrecht, Netherlands

i29 interior architects

Laser-cut geometric shapes bring depth and transparency to the ceiling-height kitchen cabinets in this Amsterdam apartment. The scattered holes (which double as handgrips) in the doors gradwelly become larger, eventually culminating in the almost-hexagon that outlines the sink and cooktop space. White spray paint for the cabinets and pinewood paneling for the recessed cooking area create blocks of color that accentuate the spontaneity of the cutout sections. Four Grcic Chair Ones pick up on the design and translate it to the dining area, creating a visual link between the two areas.

> »
>
> # LASER-CUT GEOMETRIC SHAPES ADD DEPTH AND TRANSPARENCY.
>
> «

OPERA PALACE

Istanbul, Turkey

Autoban

Design studio Autoban strike a delicate balance between revealing the original nature of a historic Istanbul apartment and modernizing it according to the needs of its new inhabitant, an art collector. After removing internal partitions to create a flowing living space in the language of a gallery, they designed the kitchen as an adaptable space: it can take part in the larger space or be partitioned off with delicate white shutters. Inside, shutters also screen off cooking tools and ingredients, leaving the marble-topped bar as a streamlined central feature.

GLEN

Cape Town, South Africa

SAOTA and Three14 Architects

Nestled into a sloped site with views of Lion's Head and Table Mountain, this Cape Town home was rebuilt for a family with teenage children. The kitchen lies at the heart of the home, beneath a large suspended wooden ceiling. A stone fireplace and raw concrete surfaces interact with integrated wooden elements and seating to create a welcoming space. Bordered by staircases, the kitchen collects the flow of circulation and orients it towards the central courtyard, which colors the interior with the light of the evening sun.

AITIO AND KERROS

Helsinki, Finland

Cecilie Manz and Matti Klenell for Iittala

Aitio means "theater box" in Finnish. Unlike their namesakes, however, the shelves in Cecilie Manz's collection put the spotlight on their contents rather than on events happening elsewhere. The playful storage solutions are made of powder-coated steel and birch wood, and feature optional plastic hooks. They can be used as individual units around the home, but work especially well when combined to form a larger system in the kitchen. Fixed to the wall or lined up along the worktop, the boxes turn pots of fresh herbs, bottles of condiments, and stacks of glasses into decorative objects in their own right. And with a variety of high-rise and low-rise versions available in a range of colors, finding the right mix to suit your style will be a piece of cake.

Kerros, a smart new member of the Iittala family, is a versatile little number that brings extra levels of storage and display space to any room in the home. It can function as a useful set of shelves for kitchen items, a two-tier side table for wine and nibbles, or an attractive stand for sandwiches and cakes at a baby shower or afternoon tea. Designer Matti Klenell describes Kerros as occupying a space somewhere between furniture and a household device—an ambiguity that brings an added, engaging layer of meaning to the unpretentious plywood design.

COOKING STORIES

AVOCADO BRUSCHETTA & PRAWN PASTA

FVF COOKS TEAM LUNCH

Freunde von Freunden is an online interview magazine that tells stories about creative individuals, documenting not only their work but also their environment and daily life. These three facets coalesce in FvF Cooks: the series of culinary encounters kicked off with a lunch by FvF's managing editor Zsuzsanna Toth and Katie Hill of the creative agency MoreSleep in the FvF Apartment in Berlin Mitte. Designed by Etienne Descloux and Katrin Greiling, the apartment has hosted everything from fashion presentations to whiskey tastings. The cooking series, however, transforms the apartment into a fully lived-in space, featuring a kitchen with Dornbracht fixtures, Miele and Dyson appliances, and a mixed collection of kitchenware. The kick-off lunch of avocado toast and prawn linguini, served to guests at Jean Prouvé's elegant EM table, surrounded by a selection of black chairs from Vitra, translated FvF's communal celebration of everyday inspiration into a multisensory experience.

» A CELEBRATION OF INTER-NATIONAL CULINARY ENCOUNTERS. «

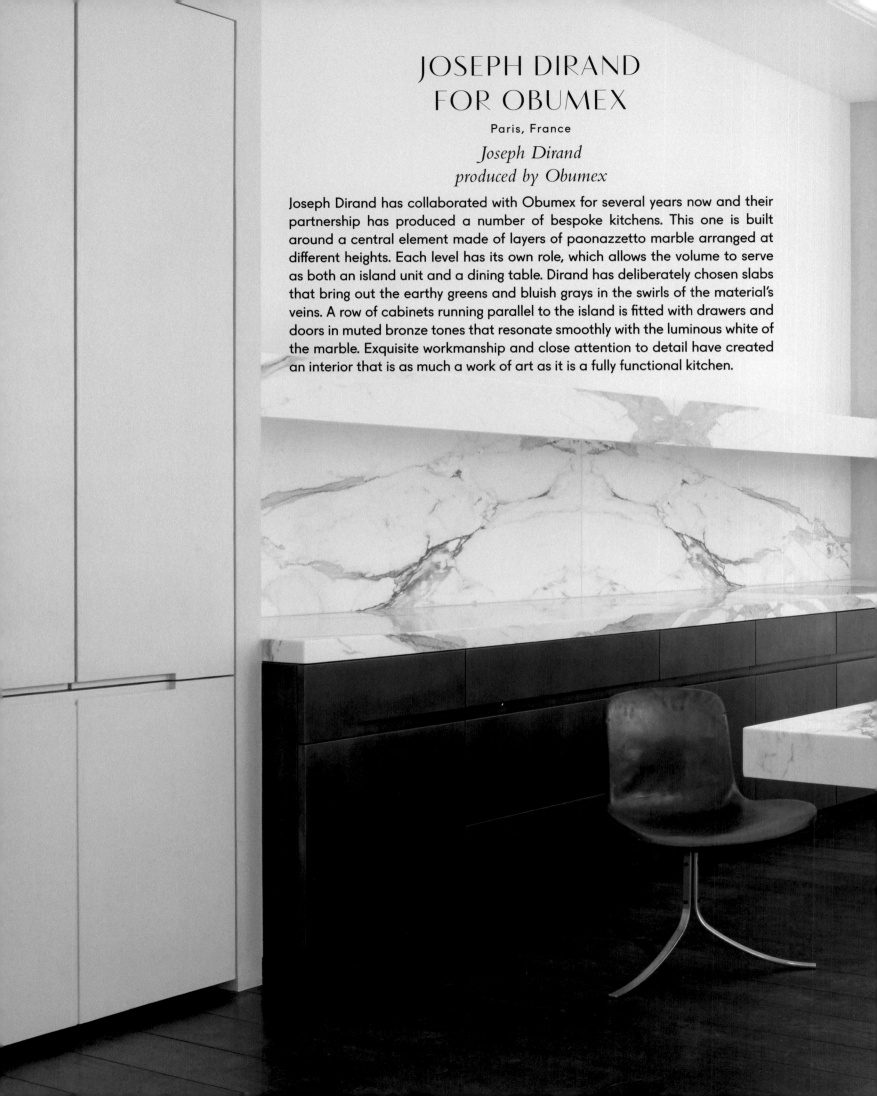

JOSEPH DIRAND
FOR OBUMEX

Paris, France

Joseph Dirand
produced by Obumex

Joseph Dirand has collaborated with Obumex for several years now and their partnership has produced a number of bespoke kitchens. This one is built around a central element made of layers of paonazzetto marble arranged at different heights. Each level has its own role, which allows the volume to serve as both an island unit and a dining table. Dirand has deliberately chosen slabs that bring out the earthy greens and bluish grays in the swirls of the material's veins. A row of cabinets running parallel to the island is fitted with drawers and doors in muted bronze tones that resonate smoothly with the luminous white of the marble. Exquisite workmanship and close attention to detail have created an interior that is as much a work of art as it is a fully functional kitchen.

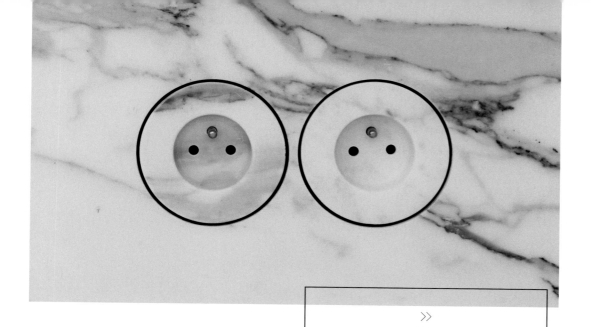

»

EXQUISITE
WORKMANSHIP
AND CLOSE
ATTENTION TO
DETAIL.

«

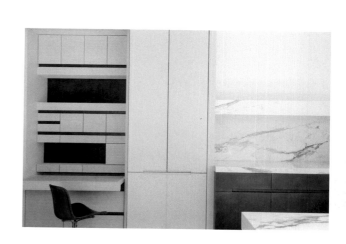

ESPACE ST-DENIS

Montreal (QC), Canada

Anne Sophie Goneau

When you enter this chic Montreal condo, the semi-closed hallway immediately guides your eye to the open-plan kitchen. Designed as the focal point of the space, the kitchen stretches the length of the sidewall and pits glossy black units and appliances against the pale white island and matching dining table. The cooktop with integrated subhood ensures that nothing obscures the red brick wall, which doubles as a splash back and is lit by LEDs recessed in the counter. Hemlock wood exposed on the far side of the kitchen units creates a tonal link to the bricks, with both functioning as visual reminders of the original materials that built this 1887 triplex.

INVISIBLE KITCHEN

Duivendrecht, Netherlands

i29 interior architects

Making a kitchen disappear sounds like it would challenge even the most dedicated of magicians, but the interior architects who designed this Paris apartment managed it. Sliding panels that are exact copies of the original walls keep the appliances and storage space so well hidden that you would be forgiven for thinking someone plain forgot to install the kitchen. The only part that is permanently visible—the island unit—gets as close to invisible as it can. It incorporates the sink, the cooktop, and all the electrical connections in a surface that looks as if it were just an inch or so thick.

THE VICTORIAN TERRACE

Colchester, United Kingdom

Jamie Blake / Blakes London

In a Victorian terrace in Essex, Jamie Blake of Blakes London unifies the kitchen through the motif of copper. A polished end panel covers one side of the kitchen island, installed below a trio of reclaimed copper pendant lamps; the black AGA cooker is topped with a copper back guard, while other small elements, from electrical outlets and door handles to antique jars and even the threads in the patterned towels, carry out the theme. The overall effect not only draws the eye around, enlivening the space, but also builds a subtle harmony between an eclectic collection of kitchen objects.

BONHÔTE HOUSE

London, United Kingdom

AOC Architecture

Bonhôte House is a four-story townhouse in Stoke Newington, London. After removing the floor in the front room to create a double-height space filled with natural light, the architects installed a brass stair leading from street level to the kitchen-diner conversion in the basement. With floor tiles arranged in irregular geometric patterns, concrete worktops that appear to levitate above the mirrored doors beneath, and polished brass light fittings that match the banisters, the kitchen is at once sophisticated and playful, luxurious yet practical. The space also features a uniquely personal touch: the team at AOC photographed each family member's profile and used them to create four different timber moldings for the wood that now lines the kitchen walls.

PROSPECT HEIGHTS RESIDENCE

Brooklyn (NY), USA

Workstead

If we told you that bright colors were the driving force behind the design for this Brooklyn apartment, you would be unlikely to believe us. After all, the walls are mainly gray, the floors are stained ebony, and a slab of black walnut from North Carolina hugs the white kitchen island. Greens, blues, yellows, and reds are nowhere to be seen. What happened was this: the owners wanted a lot of color, but they were working with designers who rarely use it. After much deliberation, the Workstead team hit upon brass as a solution. Bright enough for the owners and subtle enough for the designers, the material appears on the faucet, drawer pulls, door handles, and cooktop knobs. Its rich golden tones also make an eye-catching feature of the hood suspended above the gas range.

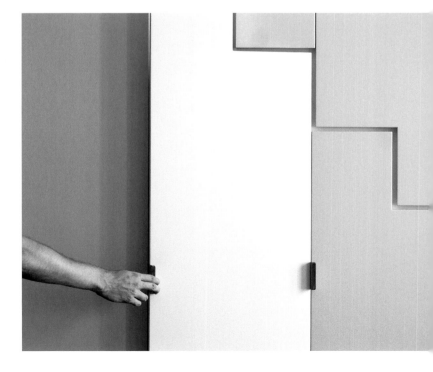

APARTMENT IN AMSTERDAM

Amsterdam, Netherlands

Mamm Design

Amsterdam is a wonderful city for many reasons, but the weather is not one of them. The family who occupy this duplex unit are used to a less gloomy climate, so they asked Mamm Design to make their home as bright as possible. The architects responded by putting the kitchen, bathroom, and bedrooms in a tower rising through the apartment. This allowed them to open up the surrounding spaces and let the light shine in. The sunken kitchen sits at the heart of a spacious living and dining area that opens onto a decked terrace. Although the design is a masterpiece of innovative architecture, the main benefit of the kitchen (if you ask anyone under the age of 12) is that it left space for a mezzanine play area in the roof.

HOUSE IN ITAMI

Itami, Hyogo, Japan

Yo Shimada / Tato Architects

When Tato Architects designed this house, they wanted to challenge the conventional division of architecture and furnishings. Stairs, laundry space, and handrails have a distinctly furniture-like quality, while sofas and closets look like archtectural elements. The concept is also reflected in the kitchen, which is built around the stairwell between the first two floors. The dining table doubles as a partial roof for the stairwell, while a kitchen unit serves as an extension of its sidewall. Although the interior design is heavily minimalist, it also features some neat, unexpected twists, such as the patterned glass on the rear panel of the kitchen unit, and the chairs bearing crucifixes and Bible storage space.

PIGEON TOE
CERAMICS

Portland (OR), USA

Lisa Jones / Pigeon Toe

Lisa Jones founded Portland-based Pigeon Toe in 2009 to bring a rich history of handicraft into contemporary products for the home. Based on a palette of white porcelain, the range of kitchenware interprets the basic functions of preparing and serving food through simple shapes, embellished with sheer glazes, woven reed, or silicone cord when necessary to contain liquid, moderate heat, or add comfort. Unexpected objects like tumblers, colanders, and mortar and pestle show the versatility of this familiar, yet endlessly surprising material.

LIFE POD

Johannesburg, South Africa

Clara da Cruz Almeida
Dokter and Misses (product design)

The life POD is a 17-square-meter prefabricated home designed for the South African context, manufactured in Johannesburg, and delivered and installed on-site. Architect Clara da Cruz Almeida and designers DOKTER AND MISSES arrange the micro-kitchen underneath the sloped roof, with laser-cut plywood and bent, powder-coated steel storage containers mounted on vertical channels above stainless steel counters. The utilities are designed for easy connection to conventional electrical and plumbing supplies or to off-grid energy generators. The life POD enables an intelligent use of resources, despite the challenges of nomadic contemporary life, for under € 14,000.

HOUSE IN HIKONE

Hikone, Shiga, Japan

Yo Shimada /Tato Architects

Kobe-based Tato Architects designed this home for a young family in Hikone. It is a white oval cylinder punctured with 42 windows and accented with hanging wooden boxes. The kitchen is built in the same visual language with a steel countertop that demarcates the work surface. Utilities, from air ducts to light cables, cross the space exposed as visual elements, while the windows form a mosaic of views of the grassland outside.

SIMPLE KITCHEN NAMED KAZE

Okayama, Japan

Michiko Yoneto for KitoBito

KitoBito, the solid wood design company based in Misaki, displays its intricate joinery techniques to the fullest in its showroom kitchen, named Kaze, or wind in Japanese. The name refers to the climatic conditions of Japanese homes, where extremely humid summers increase the stress on inflexible plywood and screw or nail joins. Here, rather, the solid oak construction moves naturally with environmental changes. The longevity of the counters, tables, shelving, and other furniture is only strengthened by the timeless, pared-down aesthetic.

TRUEHOMEWARE

Vienna, Austria

RIESS

Enamel, made of iron fused with silicate glass, has been used in commercial objects in Austria since the mid-19th century. This material was reinterpreted for historic enamel factory RIESS by Vienna-based studio dottings in the truehomeware range, combining enamel's innate beauty and practicality with the conveniences of modern life. The Aromapots work with both conventional and induction cooking; they have angled sides for stacking and a special lid that can be used at the table as a trivet for the hot dish.

TSUBOMI HOUSE

Tokyo, Japan

Yoshinori Sakano / Flat House
produced by Nagahashi Construction

In typical Tokyo fashion, architect Yoshinori Sakano has constructed a family home and biscuit shop with a footprint of only 26 square meters. A prism of angular white steel panels and glass from the outside, the home interior is built almost entirely in herringbone larch plywood panels. The rooms, arranged in seven split-levels around a central staircase, facilitate the essentials of domestic life, but still manage to be comfortable and inviting: the kitchen is a compact wall of tools, spices, and baskets, poised between the children's toy area and a tiny balcony.

B&M

London, United Kingdom

Rainer Spehl

Asked to design a kitchen with open shelving, German designer Rainer Spehl anticipated the need for a staircase and created a "staircase sculpture" in which the three functions converged. The assembly of solid and veneered oak with mahogany steps melds seamlessly with the existing oak floor and brick wall. The construction transitions from the more solid, linoleum-topped cabinets to the open boxes hung from slender posts below the staircase. Except for the stairs, produced in London, the rest of the system was pre-fabricated, flat-packed, and driven from Berlin in a small van.

PLUS ONE BERLIN

Berlin, Germany

spamroom
produced by Berlinform

The Berlin district of Neukölln is a vibrant, raw, and creative neighborhood that has definitely made its mark on the Plus One Berlin space. Plywood, old panel doors, and sections of parquet flooring combine to give the kitchen a personality much bigger than its physical dimensions. Pale pastel tiles on a cream wall let the units have the entire spotlight, which comes via fixtures made from old copper piping. A long wooden bar can function as a desk or a dining table. With the window opened wide, two people can sit opposite each other—though they might have to toss a coin to decide who gets to dine alfresco.

THE WHITE RETREAT

Sitges, Spain

Andrea Serboli and Matteo Colombo /
Colombo Serboli Architecture

Pretty much everything in this small seaside apartment is white—including, unsurprisingly, the kitchen sink. The only exceptions are the tiles that line the back wall of the kitchen compartment and the bathroom. Lifted from Superstudio's iconic 1970s Quadrena table, the black crisscross design adds texture to the otherwise smooth surroundings. To maximize the limited space and give the owner as much flexibility as possible, the architects installed horizontal sliding doors over the kitchen compartment. Although they keep it well camouflaged when not in use, the doors are easy to open whenever a balcony breakfast or sparkling sundowner is called for.

IST FAMILY HOUSE
Čunovo, Slovakia

JRKVC – Peter Jurkovič

Bratislava-based JRKVC challenged themselves to build "a small house on a small plot for a reasonable price." The resulting 85-square-meter IST house, built for €85,000, takes inspiration from the humble materials, pitched roof, small windows, and gánok (porch) of Slovenia's folk architecture. Except for the sleeping and dining spaces, every functional need is condensed into one plywood "service box" with integrated kitchen, bathroom, staircase, storage, and upper workspace, with built-in lighting and electricity. The architectural device brings organized simplicity to domestic living.

CLIMBING FRAME APARTMENT

Paris, France

CUT Architectures

The owner of this Parisian apartment grew up here, so when he returned and purchased it for his own family, he commissioned CUT Architectures to redesign the space and give it a totally different feel. Nevertheless, an element of childhood still remains in the kitchen, which features a structure that could easily be mistaken for a jungle gym. The white, three-dimensional steel grid is accessible from both sides and is linked via a doorway to a matching unit in the lounge. Wooden cabinets take up some of the cubes, while others are left empty to be used as shelves. A mobile worktop that fits neatly into one side can be pulled out so the whole family can gather round and prepare dinner together.

ALFRED STREET RESIDENCE

Melbourne, Australia

studiofour

A handsome wooden book-wall frames the archway that leads from the lounge to the linear kitchen of the Alfred Street Residence. This, combined with the raised flooring, draws a clear line between the very different functions that the two rooms serve. The kitchen's snow-white walls and units draw the eye to the elongated dining table, which becomes a workspace and breakfast bar at the far end. Tall pivot doors keep a butler's pantry and laundry hidden but also easily accessible. A section of the sidewall is fitted with ceiling-height windows that open onto the patio.

RAILWAY KITCHEN
Stockholm, Sweden
Bucks and Spurs

The Bucks and Spurs Railway Kitchen fuses rough sawn oak and smooth planed oak to create an unusual combination of clean Scandinavian lines and the rustic feel of a North American ranch. Despite the obvious lack of anything resembling a locomotive, the name of the collection actually fits like a glove. Each of the modules (drawers, cabinets, shelves, mirrors, ladders) hangs on a rail attached to the wall. Since only the rail is fixed, you are free to move things around even once your kitchen has been installed. Railway also features two larger units that can incorporate a dishwasher, stovetop, and sink, or a fridge, wine fridge, or oven. Manufactured in Sweden from the finest materials, this gorgeous collection will bring out the best in kitchens from Sacramento to Stockholm and beyond.

KL

Copenhagen, Denmark

Rainer Spehl

In a Copenhagen apartment, Rainer Spehl responded to the client's desire for a cozy kitchen by redesigning the conventional distribution of cabinets and appliances into a more relaxed landscape of functional volumes. The inhabitant can use one blue linoleum counter, for example, while chatting to someone seated across on the gray-stained oak veneer bench. Spehl dispenses with upper cabinets, instead integrating storage space into the furniture wherever possible (even behind and below the bench). The layout emphasizes visual connections and communication between its users.

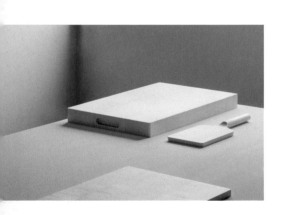

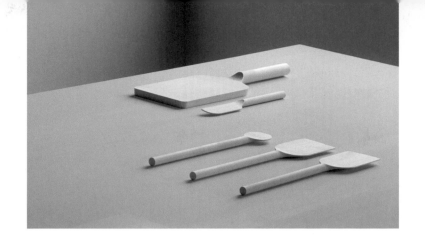

PALUTTA
Trin-Mulin, Switzerland
Carlo Clopath
produced by OKRO

Though the Palutta collection draws heavily on the manufacturing traditions, culinary customs, and styles of the Grisons region in Switzerland, designer Carlo Clopath has paired these with modern forms and elements picked up from further afield. Items that are used for eating, for instance, are coated in Japanese urushi lacquer, a durable natural lacquer that protects wood from acids, bases, alcohol, solvents, and humidity. Palutta is produced industrially and features stainless steel, porcelain, maple wood, and linen.

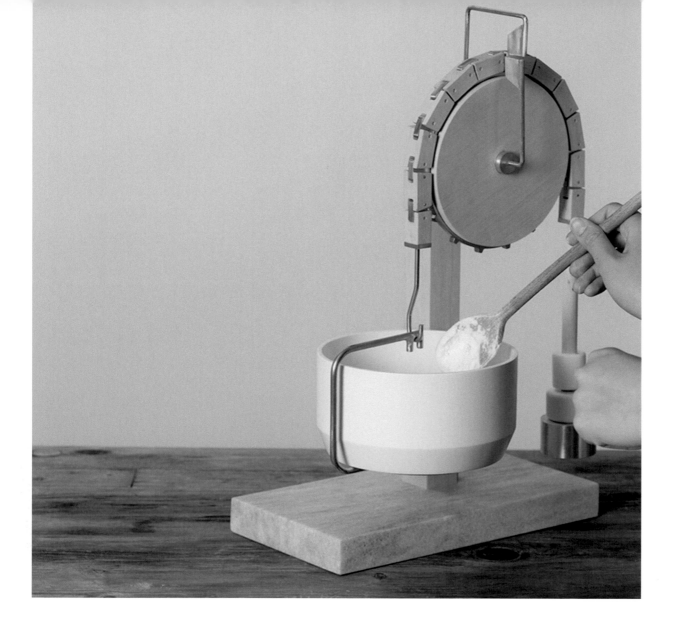

BALANCE

Lausanne, Switzerland

Nadine Fumiko Schaub

Balance is more than just a scale—it is an attempt to recreate the emotional bonds between consumers and the products they use. Nadine Fumiko Schaub, the woman behind Balance, believes that this is one way of reviving our understanding of the meaning of a product, the value it contains, and the impact it has on our lives. In contrast to the overly complex nature of modern kitchen devices, Nadine's scale features a deliberately low-tech design that means users can fully understand and directly participate in the processes that make it work. She has also chosen to make the scale out of robust, long-lasting materials such as brass, stone, wood, and porcelain, as an argument against the throwaway culture that is so damaging to the world around us.

COOKING STORIES

» FVF COOKS AT ALI SCHWARZ'S BERLIN OPEN KITCHEN «

Sabich with Haya and Nuriel Molcho & Ali Schwarz

FVF COOKS COMMUNAL DINNER

FREUNDE VON FREUNDEN
BERLIN, GERMANY

When online magazine Freunde von Freunden met chef and restaurateur Haya Molcho for their FvF Cooks series, they explored the Mediterranean-influenced cuisine she has become renowned for at Vienna's Neni and Tel Aviv Beach eateries, and has most recently brought to Zurich and Berlin via the 25hours Hotel. To celebrate this latest foray into Berlin, she hosted a communal dinner in the Kreuzberg home of Ali Schwarz, one half of DJ duo Tiefschwarz, along with their respective families. The kitchen, an eclectic mix of rustic wooden table, orange wire folding chairs, and exposed metal kitchen surfaces hung with cooking tools and assorted curios, is a perfect match for Molcho's sabich, an Iraqi Jewish dish that brings together fried eggplant, tahini, hardboiled eggs, and chopped salad in a pita bread. The event evokes the spirit of balagan, or pleasant chaos—by chance, the title of Molcho's newest cookbook.

CHÂTEAU DE LA RESLE

Montigny-la-Resle, France

Studio Roderick Vos

Château de la Resle is not only a design hotel but also a collection: the custom-made objects by Dutch designers found in the renovated Burgundy estate can also be bought. Many of them appear in the dine-in restaurant kitchen, where Roderick Vos designed everything from the clean-lined black plate steel and natural oak island to the softly beveled chopping boards in walnut and beech. In keeping with the hotel's spirit of innovative luxury, the chopping board can be hung on the wall to display its striking silhouette, or transform into a table-top on metal legs to serve aperitifs.

THE LUXURY
EXPERIENCE,
FROM BLACK
PLATE STEEL TO
NATURAL OAK.

BERLIN STUDIO KITCHEN

Berlin, Germany

45 Kilo

The guys at 45 Kilo make some of the freshest kitchen accessories around. Their Bread Box, a steel container with an oak lid that doubles as a cutting board, keeps loaves and rolls super fresh, but is also great for storing onions, apples, and the like. As for the room itself, 45 Kilo do a pretty mean kitchen. Their Berlin Studio Kitchen, for instance, features a beautiful copper worktop and replaces the usual drawers (with all their expensive runners, lacquered fronts, and handles) with recycled plastic containers. For a green alternative to paper or plastic at the checkout, simply take a container with you when you go to the store.

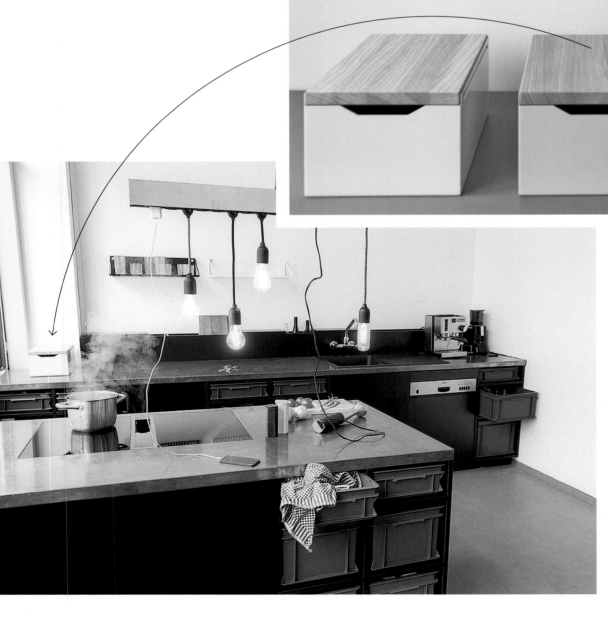

DOLMEN,
LANDO CONVIVIO

Rossano Veneto, Italy

Enzo Berti
produced by Lando

Enzo Berti's Convivio furniture makes a strong sculptural impact with angular worktops, chic cabinets, and inventive tables. Clean lines and steel enhance the materiality of the wooden pieces, which come in either walnut or larch. Unexpected splashes of color on the underside of a table or behind a sliding cabinet door bring a playful element to the collection. If you choose to have your worktop in the center of the room, you can combine it with one or more of the tables to create a one-of-a-kind layout for your kitchen.

B2 KITCHEN

Aich, Germany

bulthaup and EOOS

Kitchens are a lot like workshops. They are both places where we take disparate parts and put them together with tools to make something new. The people at bulthaup see things in a similar way, and have based their b2 kitchen entirely on the idea of a workshop. It features a work-bench (for the cooktop and sink), tool cabinet (for crockery, utensils, spices, and food), and appliance cabinet (for the oven, dishwasher, and refrigerator). The straight-talking design keeps things grounded, while the high-quality materials and outstanding workmanship ensure this shop will carry on working for years to come.

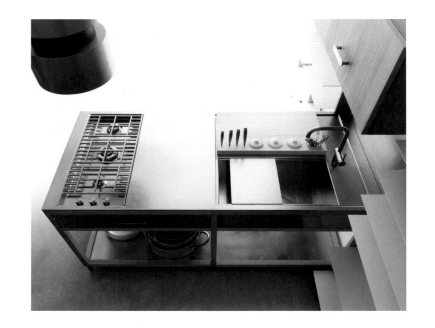

FORGIA,
LANDO CONVIVIO

Rossana Veneto, Italy

Enzo Berti
produced by Lando

The Forgia kitchen top is entirely made of steel, molded and
brushed by the hands of local Italian artisans. It can be fitted within
the structures of the Convivio line in various manners, adapting to
different spaces elegantly. The design is well thought-out down to
the smallest details, and embraces functionality through its clean
lines and minimal aesthetic.

OPENCASE WALL SYSTEM

Seattle (WA), USA

Henrybuilt Design Group

Henrybuilt proposes a way to make wall-mounted furniture easily reconfigurable through Opencase, a system of pre-fabricated wall panels offering different configurations for screw-in mounting. Rods can be attached either as hooks for hanging or as supports for spanning objects, from shelves and boxes to wall pockets and even a small bench. While offering the maximum in practical flexibility, the system also uses high-quality materials—carefully finished woods, powder-coated or stainless steel, leather and felt—to ensure the longevity that makes such adaptation both possible and desirable.

CONCEPT KITCHEN

Karlsruhe, Germany

Bureau Kilian Schindler
produced by Naber

Kilian Schindler's modular system severs the traditional ties between a kitchen and its units. Choose any or all of the five modules—work surface and range, sink, butcher's block, storage rack, and technology tower—and they will happily follow you wherever you go. The simple plug-and-play design makes it easy to assemble and disassemble the stainless steel base elements and panels, with no need for tools. Plus, the clean, uncomplicated style means that the units will look good no matter what their surroundings.

HOUSE
IN KAMISAWA

Kobe, Hyogo, Japan

Yo Shimada / Tato Architects

In redesigning this wooden house for a young couple, Tato Architects negotiate between preserving and freely interpreting traditional culture. They began by removing all nonstructural elements and pouring a new mortar floor. Wrapping the private spaces at the heart of the home in a curved plywood wall, the cooking and dining functions are distributed around the perimeter, connecting to the enveloping nature through sliding glass walls. Contemporary fixtures are simply exposed, while the kitchen island sits on an open metal frame, developing a contemporary language of structural honesty.

SHOREDITCH APARTMENT

London, United Kingdom

Ochre

This East London apartment was a garment factory in a former life. Its heritage is still very much visible today, as Solenne de la Fouchardière of design company Ochre has filled the vast space with concrete-gray tones, industrial details, and retro metal furniture. The kitchen worktop, meanwhile, has something of the sci-fi about it, appearing to almost hover in mid-air between a translucent strip of wall at one end and a single column at the other. Stool-height chairs can either make a breakfast bar of the worktop or allow cooks to rest their legs as they rinse, chop, and stir their way to a feast. The rustic wooden surface of the dining table brings a bit of country into the intensely urban surroundings, and the mismatched chairs make everything feel nice and relaxed.

A GARMENT
FACTORY IN A
FORMER LIFE.

BERGTALLSVAGEN

Stockholm, Sweden

Fantastic Frank
Interior Stylist: Thomas Lingsell

It is unlikely that any of us will ever take up residence inside an exceptionally stylish piece of graph paper—but if we did, the kitchen would probably look something like the one in this Stockholm apartment. The grid created by the white tiles and their black edges manages to be both an eye-catching feature in its own right and a subtle backdrop that allows everything else to come to the fore. Horizontal blinds on the large windows pick up where the tiles leave off and provide privacy and shade when needed. Wooden stools, brass candleholders, and bottle-green plants bring twists and turns of color to the space. Finishing touches come in the form of low-slung lamps and a crockery collection that makes sure the calm gray-and-white palette continues right through into the smallest detail.

CASA OLIVI

Tuscany, Italy

wespi de meuron romeo architects

Amid the Tuscan hills, a 300-year-old farmhouse was transformed by Swiss architects wespi de meuron into a contemporary hotel. Respecting the architectural heritage, they carefully preserved the masonry walls with their characteristic stacked structure and small windows, but inserted a new internal wooden structure and roof, thus reorganizing the space to maintain a light, airy environment. In the kitchen, this is achieved through material distinctions between the sharp steel angles of the island and hanging door and the softer white volumes containing the entrance, gallery, and staircase.

MINÀ NATURAL SKIN KITCHEN

Treviso, Italy

Silvio Stefani + R&D Minacciolo

Minà is not a here-today, gone-tomorrow kind of island. It is built to last, to stick around like a loyal companion who never judges you for burning the onions or letting the dishes pile up. The design is a daring mix of a bygone age—love those red knobs—and effortless modern style. This combination means Minà will fit into any surroundings, whether modern, traditional, or classic. Its modular format can handle everything from vast loft apartments to small urban dwellings. Minà also comes in a professional model that delivers the robust workmanship needed to stand up to the extreme demands of a restaurant kitchen.

RE-USE: RE-EXHIBIT
A NEW CONCEPT OF
RECYCLING

Milan, Italy

Weiss.cucinebianchi

Rather than seeing recycling as a way of simply reusing waste materials, Officina Weiss has reinterpreted it as a creative strategy for experimenting with unusual shapes and innovative approaches to design. This way of thinking has given rise to some brilliantly distinctive kitchen furniture that achieves the perfect mix of good looks and sustainability. Transforming old transport pallets into chests of irregular drawers is a neat way of giving them a dapper new lease of life, and bright blocks of color are always a great match for unfinished wood.

ARBORETUM RESIDENCE

Portland (OR), USA

Skylab Architecture

In this Portland family home, the diagonal architectural form is emphasized by the interior through a strong material palette, applied almost graphically in shades of black, gray, and white. In the kitchen, black wood paneling disguises storage and appliances as pure geometric volumes, echoed by the fair-faced concrete island. Reflective surfaces, from the polished metal island base and the black glass ceiling light prism to the flush steel and glass oven, play with perceptions of depth and orientation, while the mitered marble countertop quietly echoes the angles of the home.

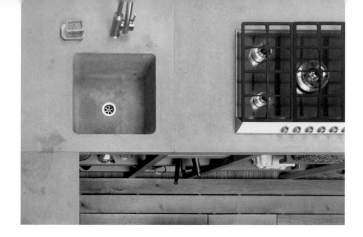

CONCRETE & OAK

Berlin, Germany

*Rainer Spehl and Alexis Oehler
produced by Rainer Spehl and betonWare*

This spacious kitchen unit exudes a raw simplicity that comes as a welcome counterpoint to the increasing complexity of our everyday lives. Berlin-based designer Rainer Spehl has twinned a solid oak frame with a concrete worktop by betonWare to create a kitchen that does exactly what a kitchen should do. It has a sink, cooktop, and loads of open storage and preparation space. The materials are sturdy and in it for the long haul. Plus, the lack of flourishes and frills creates a blank canvas that you can fill in—with ornaments, vases, plants, and lamps—exactly as you please.

INFARM

Berlin, Germany

Urban farming brought cultivation out of the country and into the city, and now crops are starting to move off the streets and into our offices and homes. Infarm, a Berlin-based start-up, is part of this movement. It develops and installs indoor vertical farms that combine efficient, cutting-edge technology with high-quality sustainable design. City dwellers often have no access to their own outdoor space, so Infarm's work is about helping them get hold of fresh, organic produce that can grow whatever the weather.

SEATTLE MINI HOUSE

Seattle (WA), USA

Michelle de la Vega

As housing becomes more expensive and space gets harder to find, many people are starting to see the benefit of downsizing to simpler, more sustainable ways of life. The Seattle Mini House shows how this can work in practice. Despite having just 23 square meters to play with, Michelle de la Vega has designed a stylish, creative, and fully functioning home. The kitchen's narrow vintage sink occupies minimal space but is still deep enough to prevent washing up becoming any more of a chore than it already is. A compact stove leaves ample room for preparing food on the countertop, and recycled wine crates provide rustic storage for crockery and other kitchen essentials below.

COOKING STORIES

ERIC WERNER

HARTWOOD

OPEN KITCHEN WITH CHEF ERIC WERNER

HARTWOOD
TULUM, MEXICO

Located along a jungle road in Tulum, Mexico, Hartwood was launched by Eric Werner and Mya Henry, two Brooklyn transplants who wanted to open a restaurant in the heart of an area with exquisite but endangered culinary traditions and local agriculture. Their colorful produce comes from communal Mayan farms, while fresh fish is spear hunted in the Caribbean; these ingredients are all cooked by hand in a wood-burning oven and open grill. Werner and Henry's innate respect for the place is evident not only in the food but also in the environment: they prefer candles to artificial lighting, use solar panels to generate the little electricity they need, and produce entirely organic compost with the restaurant waste. They have also chosen to integrate the restaurant entirely with the surroundings, forgoing a roof so that patrons can eat their meals surrounded by palm trees and tropical air.

ALHAMBRA KITCHEN

Portland (OR), USA

*Jessica Helgerson Interior Design
produced by Gregor Mitchell —
The Works Construction*

Ladders, unless you are painting and decorating, are not a common kitchen feature. If your home is a converted library, though, it seems only fair to find a way of using them. The ladder in the kitchen of Library House not only looks good, but is also fully functional and helps the owners reach the high shelves. Situated at one end of the large living space, the kitchen is overlooked by a broad window framed in the same black as the cabinets and shelves to either side. This unity of color creates a stylish bookend to the room. While the overall design mostly reflects the vintage of the house, a few modern touches, such as the curlicue desk chair and the lamps over the dining table, have been incorporated.

VINTAGE WITH
MODERN
TOUCHES.

LIBRARY HOUSE KITCHEN

Portland (OR), USA

Jessica Helgerson Interior Design

Once a narrow room with just one window to its name, this Mediterranean-inspired kitchen has been opened up, redesigned, and flooded with light. After removing the wall between the kitchen and the family room, the designers filled the resulting space with bookshelves and a built-in seating area so that it could retain its original function. At the heart of the kitchen is a high, Spanish-style island that incorporates drawers, seating, and ample space for a relaxed breakfast or lunch. A wide archway gives easy access to the dining room for more formal meals. The antique glass-fronted cabinet, moved here from the owner's bedroom, adds variety to a long wall of smart black cupboards.

PRIVATE RESIDENCE, CASTLECRAG

Sydney, Australia

Patricia Stewart Design
produced by Art of Kitchens

Australia has long been a popular holiday destination for Europeans. The antique salvage that features in this Sydney townhouse traveled the same route, but on a one-way ticket and with no need for a visa. An old French shop cabinet stands at the heart of the kitchen, retrofitted with drawers, a retractable downdraft, and induction cooktop. Two bronze Belgian lanterns illuminate the work surfaces, and traditional French doors lead into a smart storage space complete with extra sink. Additional features—including hand-painted Moroccan tiles, herringbone travertine flooring, a chalkboard splash back for notes, and polished plaster walls—bring a relaxed, timeless feel to the heart of this family home.

NW 13TH AVENUE LOFT
Portland (OR), USA

Jessica Helgerson Interior Design
produced by Hegarty Construction

If NW 13th Avenue is one of Portland's most interesting streets, then the kitchen in this petite condo is the perfect fit for its address. The rich mix of textures—from rustic red brick and stark concrete to glazed brick tiles, honed marble counters, and walnut shelves—makes for an endlessly fascinating space. Vintage Eames DKW chairs do their part by combining leather, steel, and wood, while the curved baubles of the blown-glass chandelier provide an engaging counterpoint to the right angles of the table, tiles, and windowpanes.

HOME OF NIELS STRØYER CHRISTOPHERSEN

Copenhagen, Denmark

Nathalie Schwer

When Niels Strøyer Christophersen, founder of the Frama design agency, moved from central Copenhagen to the seaside, the unrenovated apartment offered a fresh palette to create a new domestic feeling. Painted halfway up in turquoise, the walls are a muted background in which diverse materials and styles come together to make a cozy kitchen. Flea market finds and antique chairs intermingle with Frama's own F56 trestle table and AjOtto stacking stoneware vessels. As in the multicolored salvaged wood doors, the home provides a tolerant environment for unique objects to coexist.

AUTUMN/WINTER COLLECTION 2014

Copenhagen, Denmark

Broste Copenhagen
Stylist: Nathalie Schwer for Broste Copenhagen

Color is often used to tie various objects into a tableware collection, but texture, proportion, and tone families can also create harmony in more subtle ways. Broste Copenhagen's 2014 Autumn/Winter Collection shows how that can be done tastefully, matching polished wood with semi-glossy ceramic glazes and smooth white stone. Their shallow bowls and dishes can be stacked or nested to create different configurations, suggesting new ways to serve food. Their kitchen textiles bring together different hues and patterns into a single piece of fabric, wrapping the collection together.

KBH KNAST EG

Copenhagen, Denmark

Københavns Møbelsnedkeri

Kim Dolva, the founder of Copenhagen's Møbelsnedkeri (cabinetmakers), originally trained as a luthier, and the resulting attention to micro-detail is also apparent in the company's bespoke kitchen designs. Their furniture shows both an exacting approach and an intense consideration for each piece of wood, which is cut and positioned to best show off its unique beauty. From the meticulous dovetail joinery in the drawers to hand-turned knobs and carefully carved organizers, their design ethos shapes this incredibly varied material into fundamentally practical setups.

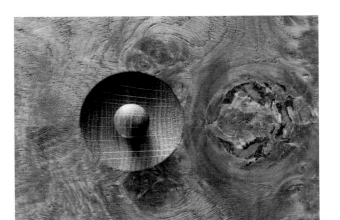

>>

ATTENTION
TO MICRO-
DETAIL.

<<

SILVER BAY

St. Helena Bay, South Africa

SAOTA

This beach villa, designed by SAOTA and Antoni Associates, reinterprets vernacular seaside architecture with modern techniques and materials. Positioned on a dune above St. Helena Bay, the open plan and panoramic glazing celebrate the incredible vista while creating a comfortable environment. Beneath the central thatched roof, three curved metal light fixtures by Okha Interiors are suspended over a James Mudge table, the salvaged wood displaying its colors at the ends, and an assortment of three-legged and turned wooden stools by Weylandts.

CUISINE
BOOG-LERICHE

Touraine, France

Elizabeth Leriche and Thomas Boog

A spacious kitchen built on split-levels, this design by Elizabeth Leriche and Thomas Boog evokes the spirit of the couple's travels and deep links to various cultures of making. One wall, for instance, features a collection of woven baskets from Zimbabwe, interspersed with Boog's own light fixtures, made of lacquered steel, bronze, and deer antlers. These more adventurous diversions are anchored by the kitchen island, an understated object made to measure by Darty and finished in matte taupe lacquer with a gray Brazilian stone counter.

OSEA

London, United Kingdom

Plain English

Although Plain English specializes in fitted kitchen units, the Osea kitchen includes an exception: its freestanding island, raised off the floor on legs, can take advantage of larger spaces to create central gathering points with ample storage and practical functions. The simple geometric shape contains unusual touches that give it a sense of history: the oak slab counter meets a sink made of slate, with antique-finish Volevatch taps reminiscent of early 20th-century laboratories, while oak-lined niches along the side of the island hold logs for a rustic touch.

I LOVE YOU MUCH
MOST BEAUTIFUL
DARLING
MORE THAN ANYONE
ON THE EARTH
AND I LIKE YOU
BETTER THAN EVERY
THING IN THE SKY.

HAMPSHIRE HOP KILN

Hampshire, United Kingdom

*British Standard
by Plain English*

Plain English balances the solidity of its cabinets with the elegance of its Osea framework to create this kitchen in Hampshire. Anchored between the solidity of the original slate floor and the worktops in solid oak or slate, the cabinets are finished with iron knobs, matching the antiqued Volevatch water taps and recalling the space's origin as a barn. The kitchen island is a lighter construction, with open shelving or perforated zinc screens covering the cabinets, while the rectangular framing echoes the half-timbered architecture.

THE REAL SHAKER COTES MILL UTILITY ROOM

London, United Kingdom

deVOL Kitchens

Founded in 1989 by two design graduates from Loughborough University, deVOL now displays its custom-made showroom kitchens in a historic 16th-century water mill. Here, the Cotes Utility Room is used to show an elegant but compact kitchen arranged along one wall, with glass and solid-fronted cupboards as well as open shelves. Painted in their deep shade of "Pantry Blue" with brass handles and hinges, the cabinets are offset by a white Carrara marble worktop. The undermounted sink, in hammered copper, adds texture and a warm tone to the design.

THE REAL SHAKER COTES MILL KITCHEN

London, United Kingdom

deVOL Kitchens

DeVOL's Shaker Kitchen showroom was so sensitively integrated into the historic, company-owned Cotes Mill that it seems to have grown with the building, despite offering the utmost in contemporary demands for efficiency and comfort. Finished entirely in pale, muted colors, the kitchen range offsets the dark floorboards and original ceiling beams, while the Silestone worktops reflect light onto the rough texture of the whitewashed walls. Glass and pale ceramic cooking and serving vessels emphasize the passage of light through the generous space.

THE REAL SHAKER KEW KITCHEN

London, United Kingdom

deVOL Kitchens

In a townhouse in the London suburb of Kew, deVOL's Shaker kitchen creates a quiet but welcoming mood through a mix of subtle design decisions and small whimsical touches. By housing the pantry, refrigerator, and tableware in a tall triple cupboard and restricting the number of glass fronts in the fittings, the beautiful wooden surfaces become a neutral background, painted entirely in deVOL's Mushroom shade (including knobs). The white Esse stove, topped by deVOL's laundry maid and clothes airer, creates a single column of visual delight.

THE REAL SHAKER
LOFT KITCHEN

London, United Kingdom

deVOL Kitchens

Beneath the pitched roof of the 16th-century Cotes Mill, deVOL's Loft Kitchen highlights the elegant proportions of its Shaker range. Set against the white brick walls, the wooden cabinets are painted in "Lead," topped with black granite worktops, and finished with chrome hardware. A tall shelf traces the contours of the room, holding small touches like a mirror with a coordinating frame and delicate flowers placed in simple glassware. A fur rug, wooden ladder, and collection of old Portuguese cooking vessels in textured terracotta add soft warmth to the ensemble.

NEW NORM DINNERWARE

Copenhagen, Denmark

Norm.Architects

Scandinavia is home to dense forests, rugged mountains, and wide expanses of tundra. Choppy seas roll onto its shores, and the seasons each have their own distinctive character and color palette. These landscapes and this climate inspired the design of the New Norm dinnerware range. The colored glazes evoke cool Nordic summers, brooding skies, and the wide expanse of the ocean. Wood and stone recall fir trees and rocky peaks. Each color and material is also designed as a backdrop to complement seasonal dishes and local produce: light blue for breezy summer meals, dark blue for fish, earthy wood for autumnal dishes, and heavy stone for herbs, root vegetables, and wild berries.

NORTHSTEAD ROAD

London, United Kingdom

Jamie Blake / Blakes London

The kitchen in this Tulse Hill home is a study in textures, reducing ornament to juxtaposed materials and construction styles. The storage is a continuous part of the architecture: one wall hosts a long line of deep drawers (avoiding the need for visible hardware), while another wall is covered in the same pale gray wood. Appliances, meanwhile, are picked out in clean white, including the refrigerator, deep sink, and Aga stove. A traditional English dresser, anchoring one end of a double row of shelves made from reclaimed scaffolding planks, creates a focal point.

THE SAWING MILL

Härnösand, Sweden

Fantastic Frank
Interior Stylist: Thomas Lingsell

The Sawing Mill in northern Sweden boasts some of the best interior design of any hostel this side of the Arctic Circle. When the people at Fantastic Frank were compiling the portfolio for its sale, they wanted to capture the uniqueness of the place. The shared kitchen—the beating heart of hostels everywhere—is an inspiring mix of urban industrialism and the rural feel you would expect from the countryside setting. Large wood-framed windows let the clear Scandinavian light spill across the sociable dining tables, patterned cushions, and bare floorboards. A pair of moose antlers sits above the black refrigerator, which matches the dark kitchen cabinets and dining chairs. With style like this, it is little wonder that Sågverket has appeared in pretty much every Swedish design magazine going.

TINY HOUSE KITCHEN

Sauvie Island (OR), USA

Jessica Helgerson Interior Design

Jessica Helgerson infuses her design process with her personal interest in sustainable building and farming. Her own family home is a case study in conscientious domesticity: the cottage of 50 square meters, remodeled with mostly reclaimed materials, features a planted green roof, high-efficiency windows, and compact storage solutions. In the kitchen, a table of locally salvaged walnut, a vintage cooking range found on Craigslist, and a wood-burning stove create a picturesque setting, while small details like the wooden range hood emphasize the unique architecture.

CHIESUOLA

Bagnaia VT, Italy

Marina Sinibaldi Benatti

This fourteenth-century Benedictine monastery near Piacenza was used as a noble residence since the 1700s, and has now been transformed into a summer home by owner Marina Sinibaldi Benatti, a relative of architect Gio Ponti. Benatti has used the cellular architecture of many small rooms to explore a wide variety of colors and materials amid an eclectic range of furniture (from Cappellini to Ikea, in addition to the original historical objects). The kitchen features a beautifully carved marble sink, not only sculptural but practical for everyday cooking and cleaning.

SUCABARUCA

Toronto (ON), Canada

Luca Nichetto
produced by Mjölk

Sucabaruca is a coffee pot that began life as a melting pot. Created by designer Luca Nichetto, who splits his time between Stockholm and Venice, the set also owes a debt to a group of collectors, ceramists, and artists who together have links to Canada, Scandinavia, Japan, Russia, and New York. Unsurprisingly, then, Sucabaruca is all about combining the modern coffee rituals of places like North America and Scandinavia with the centuries-old traditions of the drink in Italy. The pot itself was inspired by an Italian TV show from the sixties, while each color scheme takes its cue from a different country or personality. The white set references fashion designer Martin Margiela, the pastel set looks to Japanese architecture, and the bold set is a nod to the work of artist Jean-Paul Goude.

AUREOLA

Toronto (ON), Canada

Luca Nichetto
produced by Mjölk

Tea ceremonies are an important tradition in many countries in Asia. Even in places where such formal rituals are not part of the heritage, the simple act of sharing tea can still be a meaningful part of social relationships. Luca Nichetto's Aureola tea set is the product of extensive research into tea cultures around the world. It includes a tea-pot, filter, and two cups, all of which are made of fine porcelain and colored with pigments normally used for oriental lacquers. The concentric circles that decorate each piece are a visual representation of how, as the heat radiates out from the tea, so the aura and energy of those participating in the ritual (whether Japanese or Afternoon) expand to fill the room.

KITCHEN FOR
CHURCH CONVERSION

London, United Kingdom

Rupert Bevan and Harriet Holgate Interiors

Rupert Bevan Ltd. had an enormous amount of space to play with when designing a bespoke kitchen for this converted London church. A vast island unit clad in patinated brass forms an impressive centerpiece. Trolleys in bleached, distressed timber stand at either side and can function as extra surfaces or be moved and used as serving units elsewhere in the house. The drinks cabinet is fitted with hand-blown glass panels that pick up the arches present in the original architecture. Blackened steel, burnt and ebonized oak, and artisan concrete create an antique feel with just a hint of industrial chic.

HEAVENLY
INDUSTRIAL
CHIC.

SABINE FAJANA

Vienna, Austria

Sabine Fajana / VIVIDGREY

This might not be the kind of transformation you come across every day, but a fresh approach to interior design has turned a former butcher's shop into a welcoming family kitchen and dining room. The decision to retain original features such as the tiled walls, exposed piping, and bare brickwork brings a sense of authenticity to the surroundings, while a kids' wigwam and toy blackboard help usher the space into the present. Wicker baskets, curved wooden dining chairs, and relaxed textile lampshades pick up on the curvature of the ceiling and soften the straight lines that crisscross the walls.

»
FROM BUTCHER'S SHOP TO WARM FAMILY KITCHEN.
«

KARAKOY LOFT

Istanbul, Turkey

Ofist

This loft in Istanbul's hectic Karakoy neighborhood is a moment of calm, designed by Ofist with an exposed aesthetic to refer to the owner's desire for practicality and comfortable simplicity. The kitchen is based on two strips: the first is a linear element that combines a cast-concrete kitchen counter, a cantilevered dining table, and a dramatic hearth under a suspended metal hood. Along the wall, an open storage system of iron rods and hanging boxes contains ingredients, kitchen tools, and wood for the open fireplace.

RIVER LOFT BUDAPEST

Budapest, Hungary

Shay Sabag

Framed by four large white columns, the kitchen is literally at the heart of this Budapest loft apartment overlooking the Danube. An assembly of polished metallic surfaces, concrete, and exposed ductwork, the monochrome background puts the focus on the bright colors of fresh produce, spices, and hanging copper pots. The kitchen sets off the almost overpowering ceiling, a masterwork in timber construction, as well as the rough brick walls and intricately woven kilim rugs. Wine bottles are also inventively displayed on the opposite wall on a grid of copper tubes.

A KITCHEN
LITERALLY IN
THE HEART OF
THE HOME.

PIL HOUSE

São Paolo, Brazil

Studio Guilherme Torres

Guilherme Torres based his interior design of this São Paulo apartment on the eclectic tastes and collections of DJ Pil Marques and his artistic roommates. A striking population of dolls colonizes every surface, alongside unique end tables and a huge sheepskin rug. Framed against the vivid blue living room walls, the pale pink kitchen features black-and-white furniture and black ceramic tiles. Miniature penguins sit atop two shelves, while more dolls intermingle with wine glasses in a vintage curio. In the same playful mode, dishes are simply stacked on the side counter.

FUCK THE
GOOD ART
THIS IS THE
WAY WE
SEE IT

HOME AND STUDIO OF GUILHERME TORRES

São Paulo, Brazil

Studio Guilherme Torres

For his own home in the charming Jardins neighborhood of São Paulo, the Brazilian architect Guilherme Torres chose an eclectic approach to materials and styles. The open-plan kitchen displays bursts of color and graphic elements that stand out among gray walls. The skylight adds a distinct outdoor feel to the kitchen and enables trees to be part of the décor—a touch of nature that is mirrored through the use of wood for the kitchen table. The table extends into a cooktop with room for storage at the bottom. The open-plan design adds volume to a relatively compact space, and the combination of natural light along with the wooden table brings a laid-back picnic feel to the kitchen.

LARISSA

Utrecht, Netherlands

VIVA VIDA

VIVA VIDA, the Utrecht-based interior design firm, completely re-worked the interior of this farm based on their "Wonderful Life" method, emphasizing the original wooden architecture while also bringing in bright colors, mixed materials, and many visual references to nature and animals. The kitchen is a delightful mishmash of plain black open cabinets housing open wooden shelves, a vivid orange table in veneered plywood matched with motley chairs and a rustic bench, and a plethora of ornaments related to family life.

PETER FEHRENTZ
KITCHEN

Berlin, Germany

Peter Fehrentz

Although the kitchen of this Berlin apartment blends with the dining and living areas, it is very much its own space with its own identity. The striking pink cabinet doors were inspired by the color often found on the side of match-boxes. To their right stands a custom-made storage unit made of wood and steel. Anything stacked on the open upper shelves doubles as decoration and feeds into the vibrant atmosphere of the overall space. Anthracite tiles line the wall behind the solid stone worktop and match the dark shades of the flooring.

STUDIO BOOT'S HOUSE

's-Hertogenbosch, Netherlands

*Edwin Vollebergh, Petra Janssen,
and Piet Hein Eek*

When the disused Garage Lathouwers in 's-Hertogenbosch was acquired by graphic designers Studio Boot, they decided to convert it into a live-work space. Within the large open structure, Piet Hein Eek's kitchen functions as a giant screening element, completely filling the section of the building with an intricate jigsaw of cabinets. Using windows instead of traditional cupboard doors, the assembly takes on an architectural character. Accessories like a vintage farm bell, ceramic dolls, and colorful straw-wrapped jugs give the impression of a cabinet of curiosities, full to the brim.

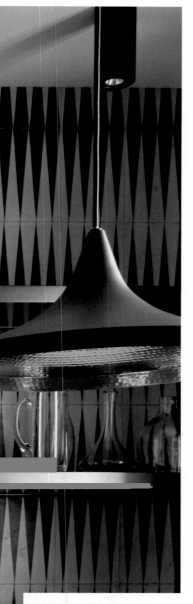

VERO-DODAT

Paris, France

Anne Geistdoerfer and Flora de Gastines / double g

The studio double g achieves a bold graphic unity in this Paris apartment, giving a fundamental language to each room and the objects within it. Black-and-white "Backgammon" tiles, handmade in Morocco for Popham Design, cover the kitchen in a striking pattern, which is reflected by the polished Zimbabwe stone worktop and echoed in the varied conical shapes of Tom Dixon's black Beat Lights, suspended overhead. The dining room, meanwhile, uses a cubist geometry of shelving and seating with bright red cushions, in dialogue with the Sonia Delaunay etchings on the wall.

AD HOUSE

São Paolo, Brazil

Studio Guilherme Torres

This São Paulo apartment was redone by Guilherme Torres to take advantage of the space in a way that reflected the owner's desire for light and integration. Some of the interventions make creative use of cheap materials to produce strong visual statements, like the ebonized wood parquet flooring or the sleek combined counter and dining table, which resembles cast concrete but is in fact made of MDF coated in the Tecnocemento cement-resin mixture. Torres obviates the need for any additional lighting by carving a linear slot of LEDs throughout the apartment that traces its way over the walls and ceiling.

REINVENTED KITCHEN

Berlin, Germany

Gisbert Pöppler

This apartment evokes an unexpected calm, given the playful diversity of furniture styles, colors, and materials that it contains. Berlin-based designer Gisbert Pöppler accented the white-walled, parquet-floored kitchen with a robin's egg blue ceiling, sea green counters, and a creamy travertine marble dining table. An antique farmhouse cabinet and dressing-room doors from the now defunct Sellbach department store contrast with modern appliances and Bruno Gecchelin's Mezzaluna lamps. The touches of brass throughout the room, from handles and taps to a custom rail for hanging cooking tools add a pleasing brightness and warmth.

FJ HOUSE

São Paolo, Brazil

Studio Guilherme Torres

Architect Guilherme Torres removed all of the partitions in this São Paulo apartment for a young DJ in order to create a new living environment, inspired by the nightclub as a closed box that gains life through the activity inside. The walls are a muted background in gray polymer cement, framing the kitchen's yellow accents, from the counter to a vintage Lambretta advertisement and blown-up photo. Screen-printed wooden stools are decoratively stored under one end of the counter for more casual gatherings, while Panton chairs at the other end devote a more formal dining area.

CRITTER MOBILE KITCHEN

Milan, Italy

Elia Mangia

Critter is a freestanding worktop that occupies the space between a primus stove and a traditional kitchen. It is made of two beams of solid wood, which accommodate the legs, and a range of interchangeable modular accessories. The whole structure is held together by just eight screws and can be disassembled in a few easy steps. Although designed as a mobile unit that can be used outside, Critter also has one eye on the home; eager for the day it can replace its conventional fitted cousin.

COOKING TABLE

Bremen, Germany

Moritz Putzier

Made of solid oak on white trestle legs, the Cooking Table looks for the entire world like a regular table. Pull the surface apart, though, and it reveals a metal track that fulfils the designer's vision of creating a flexible interplay between cooking, dining, and socializing. Gas burners can be inserted into the track and moved along to wherever they are needed. The canisters hang underneath, and a white ceramic ring fits around each burner to contain the heat and support the pans. Cooks can use the specially designed stools to either lean on as they prepare the food, or sit on when dinner is ready. A trio of bowls with chopping-board lids round off the design and are ideal for assembling and serving the meal, and for storing leftovers.

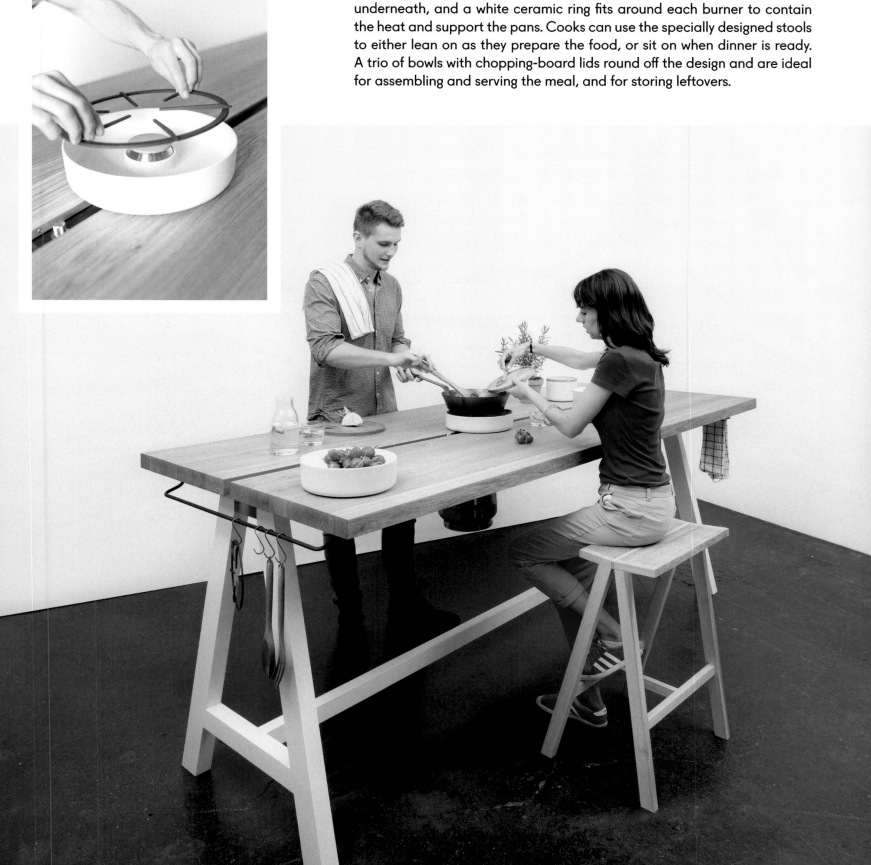

FLOW2 KITCHEN

Eugene (OR), USA

Studio Gorm

Flow2 is a living kitchen where nature and technology work together like a well-oiled (green) machine. Recycling and sustainability drive the design, which seeks to reduce waste, water use, and energy consumption. Pull back the integrated chopping board and sweep scraps directly into the worm composter. Once the worms have worked their magic, you can use the fertilizer to feed the herbs—which are watered by drips from dishes drying in the racks above. The earthenware boxes are naturally porous, so they keep bread fresher for longer and extend the life of onions and garlic. An innovative fridge box uses evapotranspiration to keep things like vegetables and butter cool, which means you can get by with a smaller refrigerator.

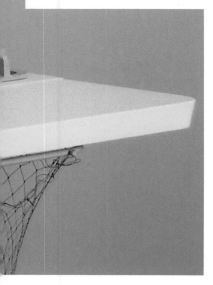

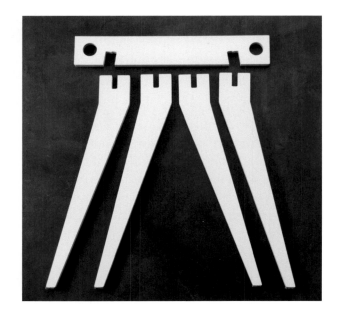

B21B

Darmstadt, Germany

Kurt Friedrich / dialog-plan
produced by p&p

Kurt Friederich's B21b kitchen strips everything back as far as it will go. The minimalist design gives users total freedom to experiment and adapt the bench to suit their needs. A sink and cooktop come as standard, but everything else is up to you. Birch multiplex and a robust Resopal surface make for a sturdy structure that is perfect for offices, apartments, and vacation homes. On a less material note, the B21b aims to focus attention on the act of buying groceries, preparing them, and eating together. This should lead to a deeper understanding of the economic and environmental impact of our choices, and help us assess where we stand within the consumerist society we inhabit.

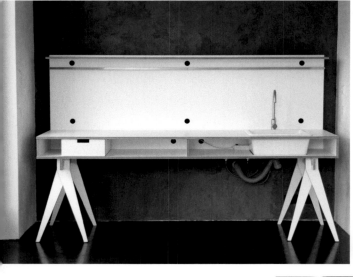

CHOPCHOP.
EASY COOKING.

Berlin, Germany

Dirk Biotto

Few of us probably think much about the fine motor skills and strength needed to prepare a meal, but these things can present a whole range of challenges for elderly and disabled people. Dirk Biotto's ChopChop kitchen module is all about removing these problems and providing an innovative approach to dinner. The design packs numerous solutions into one compact unit. They include a frame that allows you to adjust the countertop to your height, an extendable hose that brings water to where it is needed, a sloped sink that makes it easy to pull (rather than lift) things in and out, and an embedded grater and milled groove that mean you can grate carrots and butter bread one-handed.

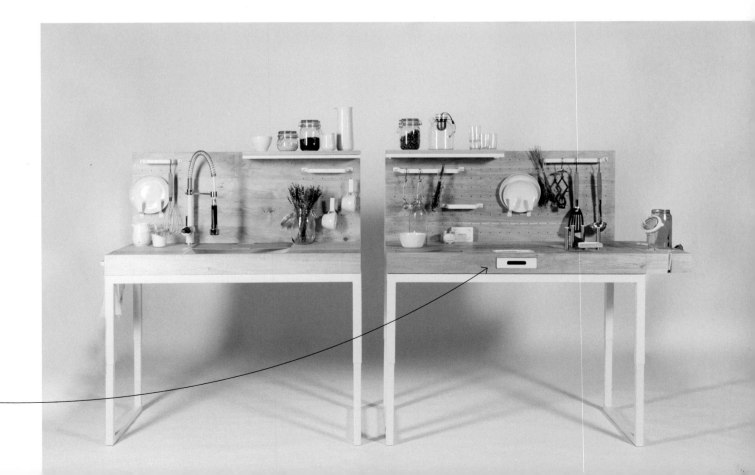

MICROBIAL HOME

Eindhoven, Netherlands

Philips Design

Reducing our environmental footprint is one of the biggest challenges of our times. Philips believes one of the solutions may lie in biological processes, since they are not particularly energy hungry and do not generate pollution. This line of thinking culminated in the Microbial Home, a proposal for a domestic ecosystem based on filtering, processing, and recycling things that we would normally consider as waste.

Instead of drawers and cupboards filled with pots and pans, the Microbial Home's island unit contains a fully functional biodigester. It converts bathroom waste solids and vegetable trimmings into methane gas, which supplies the island's integrated cooking range, powers its overhead lights, and warms the water for the home. The Microbial Home also includes a larder concept that keeps food fresh using natural processes. The designers have paired vegetable storage compartments with a twin-walled, terracotta evaporative cooler built into a dining table, encouraging a sociable approach to preparing dinner.

ECOSYSTEM-FRIENDLY INNOVATIVE DESIGN.

COLLABORATIVE COOKING MACHINE

Stockholm, Sweden

*Petter Johansson Kukacka and Christian Isberg,
in collaboration with Lasse Korsgaard and Carl Berglöf*

Collaborative Cooking is a project dreamed up by two creatives, one programmer, and a chef. They wanted to explore the future of the way we talk about and prepare food. Does a chef actually have to be present at the stove, or is it now possible to prepare a dish through the wonders of the digital world? On a quest for an answer, the team built a cooking machine that they hooked up to an online platform. The machine has six functions and space for 35 ingredients. Five chefs can collaborate on a dish, with all of them controlling the machine remotely. The system also documents each of the cooking steps so that, if the result tastes good, anyone can recreate it.

PLAT'EAU

Berlin, Germany

Lisa Keller

With the Plat'eau, Lisa Keller has devised an ingenious solution that breaks down the traditional division between sink and worktop, and brings greater flexibility to the kitchen. You can rinse carrots or plates straight under the running water, or leave a sweater to soak in one of the bowls overnight. The bowls come in different sizes and, because they are fitted with plugs, you can move them around and empty the water without tipping them up. When the Plat'eau is dry, it is perfect for chopping vegetables, making pastry, and kneading dough—plus, the proximity of the faucet is a boon for the messier cooks among us.

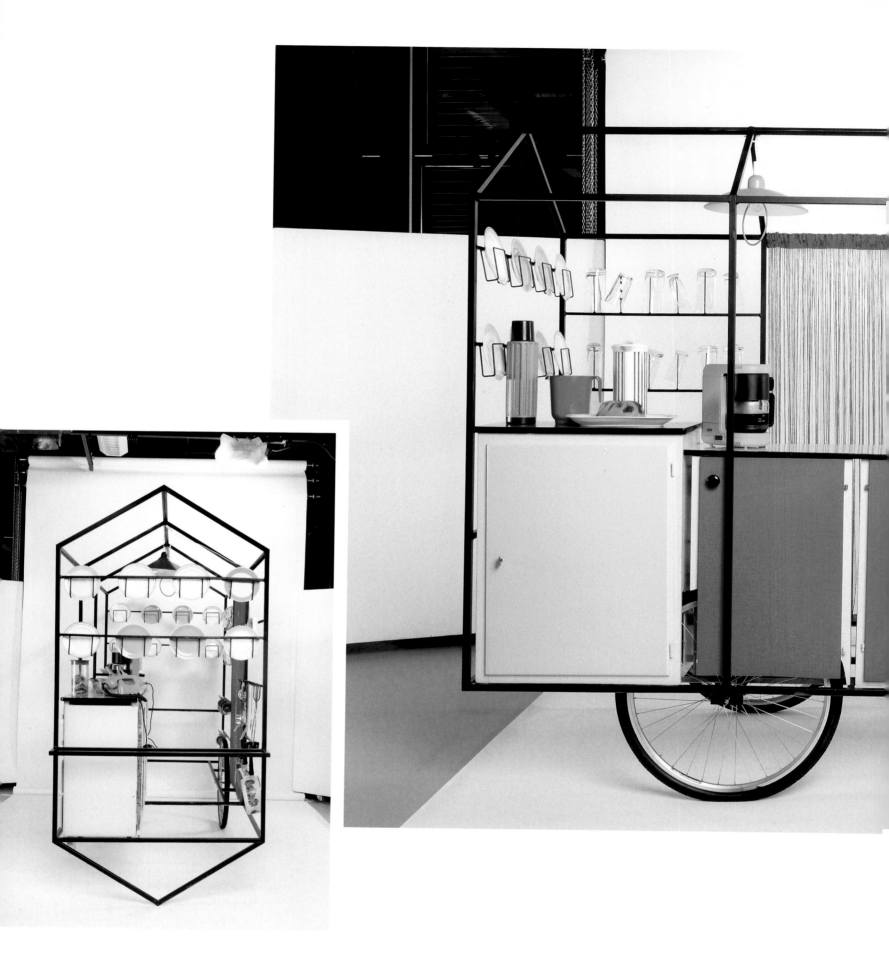

SICLI

Geneva, Switzerland

BUREAU A and HEAD

BUREAU A worked with students from the Geneva University of Art and Design to come up with new approaches to creating an exhibition space in a modern landmark building in Geneva. Inspired by the spontaneous structures and intelligent mobile designs that they had seen around the world, the group devised a series of portable modules that question the traditional white-wall, white space approach to exhibition design. The mobile café unit boasts cheerful primary colors, symmetrical crockery racks, and plenty of countertop space for cookies and cakes.

SHEPHERD'S HUT

London, United Kingdom

British Standard by Plain English

This shepherd's hut has come a long way from its days as a shelter for Victorian herdsmen. Decked out to showcase British Standard's off-the-shelf units, it is now a welcoming kitchen complete with wood burning stove. The cupboards are a tribute to honest, unfussy British craftsmanship, and the hut proves you can fit oodles of style into the smallest of spaces. Products of this quality usually come with a hefty price tag, but thanks to designer Katie Fontana's decision to dispense with the frills (like delivery and fitting), the beautiful collection is affordable to those on even modest budgets.

BLOCKBOWL

Edmonton (AB), Canada

Geoffrey Lilge
produced by OnOurTable

In founding the company OnOurTable, Canadian designer Geoffrey Lilge took inspiration from his wife's restaurant in order to create a series of beautiful objects that could live up to the extreme demands of the commercial kitchen. The BlockBowl is their first hybrid product, a two-sided cutting block in solid edge-grain black walnut. Held one way up, it features a lipped, shallow bowl for serving nuts, olives, or other small snacks; flipped over, it is a raised board for cheeses and charcuterie. Both sides use the innate richness of the material to offset its contents.

GLOW

Rotterdam, Netherlands

Agustina Bottoni

Argentinean designer Agustina Bottoni maximizes the luminance and heat potential of a small tea candle to prepare tea in a dramatic, yet unexpected way. Bottoni's tea kettle, rendered as a spherical glass bulb, brews slowly over several hours while also acting as a lens and magnifying the candlelight. The base, made of turned wood and cork, allows the kettle to be tilted in any direction for pouring, and the matching teacup is also equipped with a cork sleeve for insulation. The tea service reinvents the basic process as a contemplative ritual for the present day.

A LA CARTE

Stuttgart, Germany

Linda & Oliver Krapf /
STADTNOMADEN

Everyone knows a menu with a few select dishes on it will be much better than one that gives War and Peace a run for its money. The team at Stadtnomaden have applied that idea to their A la carte kitchen range. Its small collection of sleek white units gives today's urban nomads the versatility they need and the high quality they want. The modules can be combined to fit into any home, office, or event space. They work as islands, as room dividers, or flush against the wall, and can incorporate drawers, ovens, or dishwashers. Adjustable feet and optional castors provide flexibility, while discrete notches double as handles and cable runs. Chopping and draining boards slot into gaps between the units, and can even make space for a herb garden.

FOODLAB

Warsaw, Poland

Tomek & Gosia Rygalik / Studio Rygalik
produced by Siemens

Warsaw-based Studio Rygalik designed FoodLab as a system of mobile culinary devices that reinterprets the concept of the kitchen to meet the contingencies of contemporary life. A collaboration with Siemens for the Concordia Taste restaurant in Poznań, one of Poland's design centers, the kitchen is composed of modular units that can be easily rearranged for different functions or events. The wooden boxes, mounted on wheels, blend storage, working surfaces, water utilities, and appliances from Siemens's eco-friendly studio-Line range.

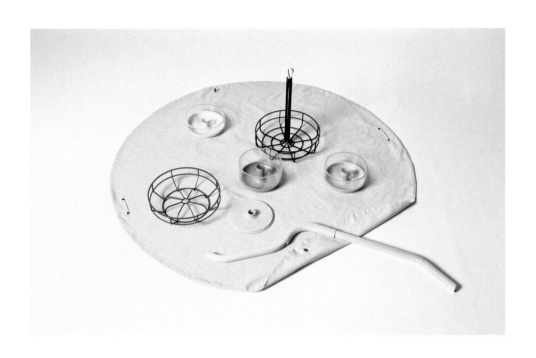

URBAN PICNIC

Amsterdam, Netherlands

Jody Kocken

Towns and cities in the Netherlands are full of lush green spaces that make wonderful settings for picnics. With that in mind, Jody Kocken developed the Urban Picnic, an updated version of the stick and kerchief once used to carry belongings on the open road. In her design, the stick is curved to sit comfortably on your shoulder, and the fabric carries the stackable containers that contain your packed lunch. Once you have found the ideal spot, untie the bundle, spread it out as a tablecloth, and dig in!

BREAD FROM SCRATCH

San Francisco (CA), USA

Mirko Ihrig

In Bread From Scratch, Mirko Ihrig reacts to the distance between everyday life and the production of our most basic foods. Although bread is one of the oldest and most universal forms of food, it is rarely made at home in the industrialized world. Ihrig's solution is a collection of objects for making bread from scratch, including a stone mill to grind flour, a jar for sourdough, a mixing bowl, a board to knead dough, and a paddle to transfer loaves into the oven, a design that combines a traditional ceramic oven with an efficient plastic base and turned wooden legs.

ETKØKKEN

Aarhus, Denmark

Mette Schelde

EtKøkken distils the kitchen down into its three most basic functions: preparation, cooking, and washing up. The units were inspired by fire pits and their ability to bring people together in a sociable circle. Blackened steel provides the framework in each case and supports solid oak for the chopping block, marble terrazzo for the sink, and a contemporary criss-cross pattern of steel for the cooker. All three are fitted with a curved rail that can accommodate the necessary utensils. While the washing station has to be connected to a water supply and drainage, the other two stations are on castors, which means they can be moved around as needed and even used outside.

TINOZZA

Treviso, Italy

Minacciolo

The Tinozza range is a perfect example of Minacciolo's knack for updating traditional designs in a way that stays true to their roots. Strips of oak wood hugged by bands of black steel recall washtubs of the past, while the elegant surfaces and smart hidden storage spaces make the units a stylish addition to any modern-day kitchen. Tinozza comes as a sink, cooktop, and work surface. Each version features elements (like the old-school red knobs) that link them to the rest of Minacciolo's portfolio. This means you can mix and match to create an eclectic, yet perfectly coordinated kitchen.

THE KITCHEN

Warsaw, Poland

Tomek & Gosia Rygalik / Studio Rygalik

Studio Rygalik originally created The Kitchen project in collaboration with a rapeseed oil brand and a bakery for the 2012 Łódź Design Festival. The unconventional set-up encourages visitors to adopt an experimental and playful approach to preparing their food. Using a basic language of bent metal tubes, each object combines a ring with four legs and various attachments. In one construction, a basket of bread is clasped between a stool and a cutting board, while another suspends an oil drip from an IV stand over a metal salad bowl. A hairdryer is also provided as an ad-hoc heating element.

251

Index

Imprint

Kitchen Kulture

CONCEIVED, EDITED, AND DESIGNED BY

Gestalten

EDITED BY

Michelle Galindo, Sven Ehmann,
and Robert Klanten

PREFACE BY

Noelia Hobeika

TEXTS BY

Jen Metcalf and Tamar Shafrir

PROOFREADING BY

Bettina Klein

COVER PHOTOGRAPHY BY

Joanna Maclennan Photography

BACKCOVER PHOTOGRAPHY BY

Wolfgang Stahr (left top); Antony Crolla (left bottom);
Lincoln Barbour (right top), and Yvan Moreau (right bottom)

ART DIRECTION BY

Studio Hausherr

GRAPHIC DESIGN BY

Jeannine Moser

TYPEFACES:

Vanitas by Michael Jarboe; Fugue by Radim Peško; Bembo by Aldus
Manutius, Francesco Griffo, and Frank Hinman Pierpont

PRINTED BY

Printer Trento s.r.l., Trento, Italy
Made in Europe

PUBLISHED BY

Gestalten, Berlin 2015
ISBN 978-3-89955-557-8

2nd Printing, 2016